NAZARTH

NAZARTH: Pillars of Gladness

ISBN 978-1-914166-44-0 (HB)
ISBN 978-1-914166-45-7 (PB)

First published in 2022.
Hadean Press Limited
Unit 30, Mantra House
South Street, Keighley
West Yorkshire
BD21 1SX
England
www.hadeanpress.com

NAZARTH

Pillars of Gladness

or

A Geomancer's Angelical Psalter of Calls,
containing vessels 19 with which
to water the Earth

Alexander Cummins

Contents

NAZARTH

On Angelical Geomancy

Wisdom sitteth upon an Hill, and beholdeth the four Winds, and girdeth herself together as the brightness of the morning, which is visited with a few, and dwelleth alone as though she were a Widow.

—Meric Causabon, *A True and Faithful Relation of What Passed for Many Years Between Dr John Dee and Some Spirits* (London, 1659)

Poetry requires no explanation, and these calls will speak for themselves with tongues *ag cormpo*, 'which none hath yet numbered'. Yet a few opening remarks to welcome, gladden, and stir the reader – as we would any other visiting spirits – are nevertheless apt to make. As this is a geomancer's psalter of Angelical calls, it is fitting to speak briefly but welcomingly of the Angelical tongue, the Geomantical oracle, and the prayerful *Commah* – that is, the 'trussing-together' – of these arts.

The Angelical Language

The Angelical language is truly Adamical: the angel Ilemese describes this sacred speech as "a language taught in Paradise… by infusion, to Adam" (*Five Books of Mystery*, p. 354). It is the tongue spoken in the Garden by the First Man and First Woman. It is thus an internationally sacred form of ritual speech, surpassing the very national borders and imperial boundaries its early modern receivers sought to impose on the world through its resort and deployment.

It is conceived of as a – indeed *the* – natural language: the most accurate and incorruptible tongue whose pre-lapsarian virtues allow it to potentially articulate (a return to) Edenic perfection. The archangel Gabriel explained to Dr Dee that Adam "not only did know all things under his Creation and spoke of them properly, naming them as they were, but also was partaker of our presence and society, yea a speaker of the mysteries of God, yea, with God Himself." (*True and Faithful Relation*, p. 92) Adam not only named the flora and fauna of Eden in the Angelical speech, but conversed with and *swore with* them in this sacred language. Raphael affirms that Adam "named all things (which knew it) and they are so indeed, and shall be forever." (*FBM*, 267) It is therefore an ancestral language, not merely in the sense of being a common treasury of all humanity, but of the whole living world and all its denizens great and small.

It is a divinely-imbued conjuring tongue, a ritual *lingua originali* which many (perhaps indeed *all*) spirits are able to understand and in which legions and hosts alike can converse. As the archangel Gabriel specified, "so are the creatures of God stirred up in themselves, when they hear the words wherewithal they were nursed and brought forth: For nothing moveth, that is not persuaded." (*TFR*, p. 92) Indeed, all of nature hears and responds to the Angelical speech. As Raphael explains "... respecting our Creation... the waters shall stand, if they hear their own speech. The heavens shall move, and shew themselves, when they know their thunder. Hell shall tremble, when they know what is spoken to them." (*FBM*, p. 267) Truly, it is a *universal* language.

It is also worth noting that the Angelical language, outside of any other ritual systems channeled by Dee and his seers, is arguably the most self-contained and complete element of the so-called Enochian magics. No missing pages or incomplete sets of sigils trouble its use. While there may be debate over the exact cosmological effects that the Angelical keys unlock, there are no real ambiguities of application. The spirits, as we read and can cite, are uncharacteristically clear and direct about its origin and potency. This is the original speech of Creation, and all things will respond to it. Prayers and other divinely-charged magical speech acts are poetries of the numinous articulated into, out of, and simply *as* the world. And to consider speaking-the-world and worlding-speech is of course also to consider *divining*.

Geomancy

Geomancy is a computational oracle of divination. Like the forms and conceptions of our numerals themselves, it is based in the Arabic sciences at the algebraic heart of so-called Western mathematics and computing, ever transforming marked sand into circuits.

The sixteen four-bit binary figures that constitute the popular geomancy of the European Renaissance apply astrological understandings to earthly lots in a dialectic of elemental transmutation. Geomancy does not simply divide up a taxonomic pantheon of distinct 'savours' of virtue as with the twelve zodiacal signs, but rather directly charts the inter-relational alchemies of these lots of fate's interactional syntheses. The Moon's dynamism of spirit (Via) will *always* lead the Young Warrior (Puer) along its winding path to Sagehood (Albus), just as Sorrow (Tristitia) will *always* remind the Lover (Puella) that grief is love persisting past mortality (Amissio). These are the empiricisms of energetic exchanges – simply *how those patterns play out* – mapped in the singled and doubled starry points of the earth that make up geomancy's sixteen-fold conceptions and articulations of the cosmos and its unfoldings.

Geomancy thus proffers much to the mystic, *in-spired* to breathe with Robert Fludd's conception of the *anima mundi* revealing the mysteries of the Highest to those with sufficient pious tranquility of soul. Geomancy also presents potent angelological spiritwork, as in John Heydon's invocations of the

Ruling Spirits by name and sigil to move the hand of the operator and give answer.

In understanding the arising and affectivity of the figures, we may not only chart transfigurations but actually *shepherd* intentional changes through operative geomantic sorcery from manipulated sortilege, and especially via talismanic ensigilisation (such as in the Solomonic pentacles) for the figures themselves are indeed 'betwixt image and character'.[1] For from these forms – these haunted doorways of possibility and the sigil nets that bind what is called forth from them – what new coherencies of reality may be ushered?

Angelical Geomancy

The historical record holds at least one explicit example of the combination of geomancy with the Angelical language – indeed, the proper celestial script of the Angelical tongue – in the form of the angelical-geomantic lettrism attributed to "Dr Rudd". What may appear at first a simple matching exercise – the corresponding of Angelical letters to the sixteen geomantic figures, or, as it is entitled in the Harley 6482 manuscript, 'The Characters of the Sixteen Figures of Geomancy Expressed in the Great and Lesser Squares of Tabula Sancta' – in actuality reveals

1 For the figures themselves are indeed "betwixt Images and Characters…" (Agrippa, *Three Books of Occult Philosophy*, p. 309).

depths of what we might call a 'geomantic *gematria*' yet to be fully plumbed.

Take for instance the Angelical word for 'joy', *moz*: spelled out, by the strange pronunciation of Angelical letters, 'Tal-Med-Ceph'. This string of letters is corresponded to Tristitia, Puella, and Fortuna Minor, respectively. And might we not say that joy is, *inter alia*, an endeavour of crafting the sorrows of the world into little victories? Such celestial geomantic lettrism also holds out further possibilities for experimentation and reflection when combined with the techniques of scrying the very Angelical letters themselves advanced by both historical and contemporary practitioners.

Speaking more broadly, three further points of engagement between the oracle and the language – and their attendant sorcerous contexts – present themselves: reading right-to-left, elemental overlay, and prayerful incantation. Firstly, and perhaps most simply, both the Angelical script and a geomantic shield chart are set and read in a reversal of the typical English left-to-right order, the latter as a survival of or perhaps homage to the oracle's Arabic roots and the former considerable in relation to Hebrew sinistrodextral orthography. And, if we are to consider the works of geomancy and the magics of the Angelical tongue, we might well note both traditions employ a great deal of 'stacking' elements upon-elements. Whether the speaking of the Airy Subangle of the Table of Water, or weighing the virtues of an Earthy figure in a Fiery Daughter's position in a geomantic shield, there is a shared conception of latticing elementist understandings;

mapping, managing, and manipulating layers of compounding affectivities.

The Angelical geomantic calls of this pocketbook are also of course much in keeping with the chief magical tool and sorcerous modality of Dr Dee and his various scryers: ardent prayer. These calls might be considered further keys to open kabalistic gates; yet outside of any particular emanationist cosmo-visions and appeals to empyrean realms, they are certainly (also) prayerful vibrational proclamations to allure and cohere the spirits and virtues of the figures themselves upon and around the sublunary earth.

Finally, 'Enochian' as a tradition of innovation certainly seems able to stand the pressure of adapting to the needs and proclivities of the various magi who have employed it and experimented with it across history. We may of course note the numerous alterations, developments, and colourful complications of the Enochian magics of the Hermetic Order of the Golden Dawn; but we may also consider the pre-modern experimentations of various conjurors and groups succeeding Dr Dee – the Angelical *goetia* of the previously-mentioned Harley manuscript, the experiments of Elias Ashmole with the Sixteen Good Angels of Physick, the instances of Angelical names and terms cropping up in seventeenth-century conjurations as words of power, as well as the scant notes about the 1688 working group who rediscovered Dee's work and sought to develop it.

Indeed, by the account of one modern authority on Enochian magic, Benjamin Rowe – an elder now passed into *Salman Teloch* (the House of Death) – it seems these Angelical magicks may encourage or even rely on the adaptations of individual operators and sodalities for their very applications:

> *Given the bare-bones nature of the original Enochian material, magicians have to improvise extensively to make it into an effective general-purpose magickal system. The history of the system's use is a history of innovation. Every magician or group that has used it extensively has added their own distinct character to it, taking it in a direction at least slightly different from anyone else. It has evolved as the viewpoints of its users have evolved, and seems perfectly capable of adapting to many viewpoints without stress.*
> —Benjamin Rowe, *Enochian Magick Reference*, p. 25

And so in the spirit of this tradition of innovation, finally, it is pertinent to speak briefly of the title of this modest psalter you hold and read from in this moment, which is dubbed *Nazarth*. Consistently, the delivering angels consider the Angelical tongue – and its formulated calls – as both water and the vessels by which to hold and pour forth water. This pocketbook of calls is thus named after a versicle from the Fifth Key: *amipzi nazarth af od dlugar zizop zlida caosgi tol torgi*, "I have fastened pillars of gladness 19 and gave them vessels (with which) to water the earth with her creatures". We should recall that when Raphael first begins to teach Dr Dee of this celestial mother tongue, this archangel – who is the Healer of God – describes the Angelical language as a liquid, an elixir, a dew, a 'Divine Medicine', and a vessel: for 'what water recreateth more, or cooleth ignorance deeper than the knowledge of our Celestial Speech?' (*FBM*, p. 267)

And thus I dedicate these pillars of gladness to you, dear reader, that they may be fonts of medicine as well as mystery. May the vessels of these calls pour forth cooling blessings of gladness at the mysteries of Creation for you as they have, do, and will continue to for me. May the waters of joy be the waters of understanding. *Mozlilzom.*

Dr Alexander Cummins
Manchester, New Hampshire
2022

[illegible]

[illegible]
[illegible]
[illegible]
[illegible]
[illegible]
[illegible]
[illegible]
[illegible]
[illegible]
[illegible]

Erm Iadnah

Argedco!
Dooaip qaal, zamran obelisong
pugo plapli ananael qaan
erm iadnah
od luciftian cors ta vaul zirn
tooat gmicalz om lrasd tofglo
odo cicle!
Zacar od camliax
qcocasb obelisong
iaial ednas cicles

The Ark of Knowledge

"With Humility We Call Thee, with Adoration of the Trinity"!
In the name of the creator, show yourselves as pleasant deliverers
as unto partakers of the secret wisdom of your creation
with the ark of knowledge
and with ornaments of brightness such as work wonders
furnishing powerful understanding to dispose all things
open the mysteries of your creation!
Move and speak
the contents of time as pleasant deliverers
conclude us as receivers of your mysteries

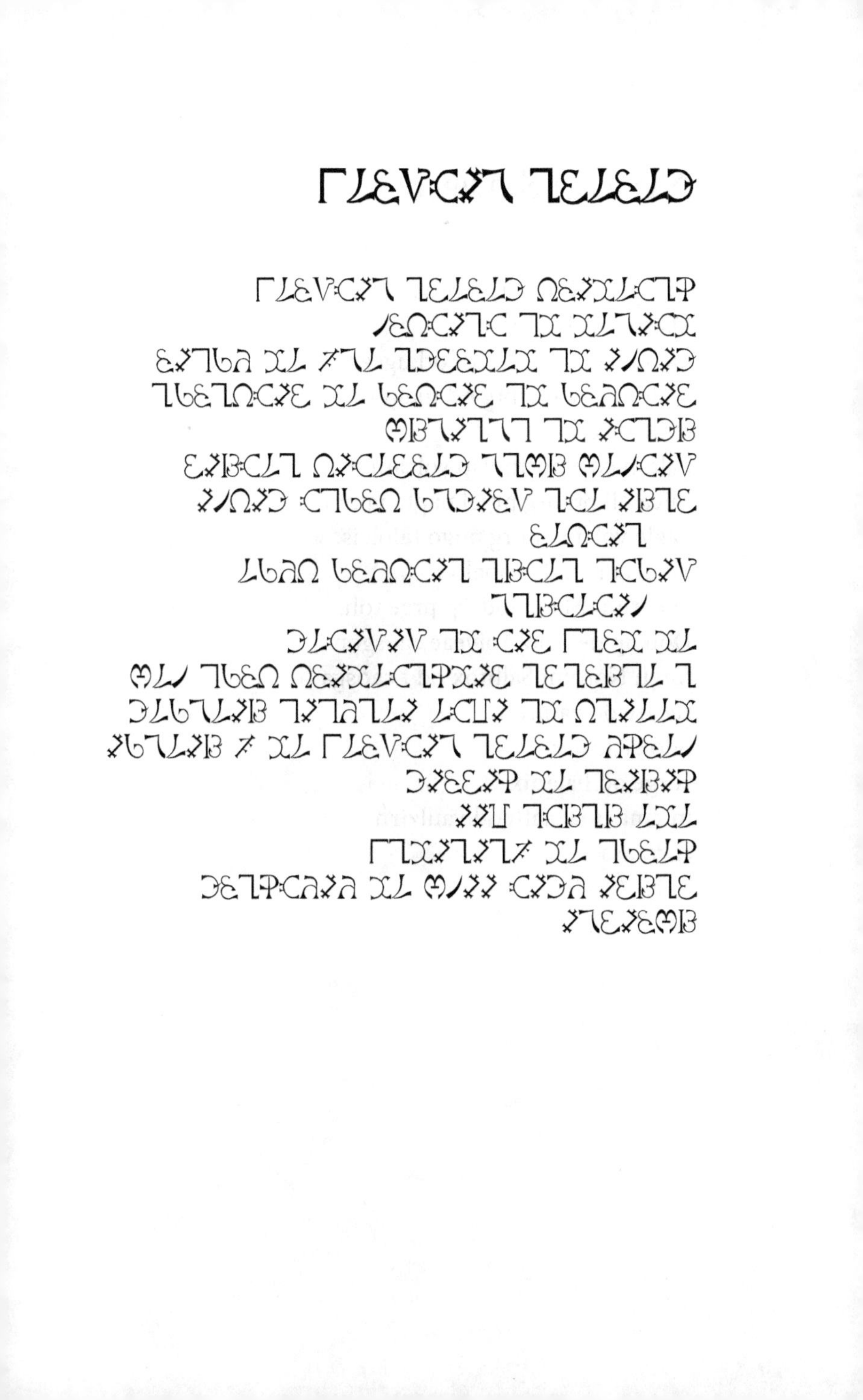

Noromi Salbrox

Zilodarp Noromi Salbrox
Dlasod de Lialprt
napta de dodrmni osf od ugear
malpurg de malprg od malpirgi
cnila de esiasch
baltoh chis normolap yolcam
mica oli bransg prgel napta ialpor
bagle yolci Ialpurg pugo talolcis,
od drix mal de babalon
i oecrimi Madzilodarp prge toh.
Dooaip de aqlo Aoiveae caosgon
torzu Noromi Salbrox od f caosga
zacare od zamran
odo cicle qaa
zorge od fiaiadix
micma unal aath od vaulzirn
chramsa

Sons of Live Sulphur

Stretch forth ye Sons of Live Sulphur
Alchemical Sulphur of the First Flame
two-edged sword of vexed discord and the strength of men
the fiery darts of through-thrusting fire and the fires of life and increase
blood of brothers
in righteousness are the sons of men who bear
a mighty guard of fire with two edged swords flaming,
for to bring forth the Burning Flames as unto bucklers
and cast down the arrows of the wicked
is to sing praises to the God of Stretch Forth and Conquer in the flames' triumph.
In the Name of your Stars unto the Earth
arise you Sons of Live Sulphur and visit the earth
move and show your selves
open the mysteries of your creation
be friendly unto me and visit with honour
behold these deeds and work wonders
be it made with power

SONG OF [illegible] DELIVERY

Stand forth ye Sons of Love [illegible]
Alchemical [illegible] of the Elder Temple
two-edged sword of good [illegible] and the strength of

[illegible] through [illegible] and the river
of life and the [illegible]
blood of brothers
[illegible]
mighty [illegible]
[illegible] burning [illegible]
and cast down the [illegible] of the [illegible]
is to sing praises [illegible] Land of [illegible] North and
[illegible]
in the Name of [illegible]
[illegible]
earth
[illegible]

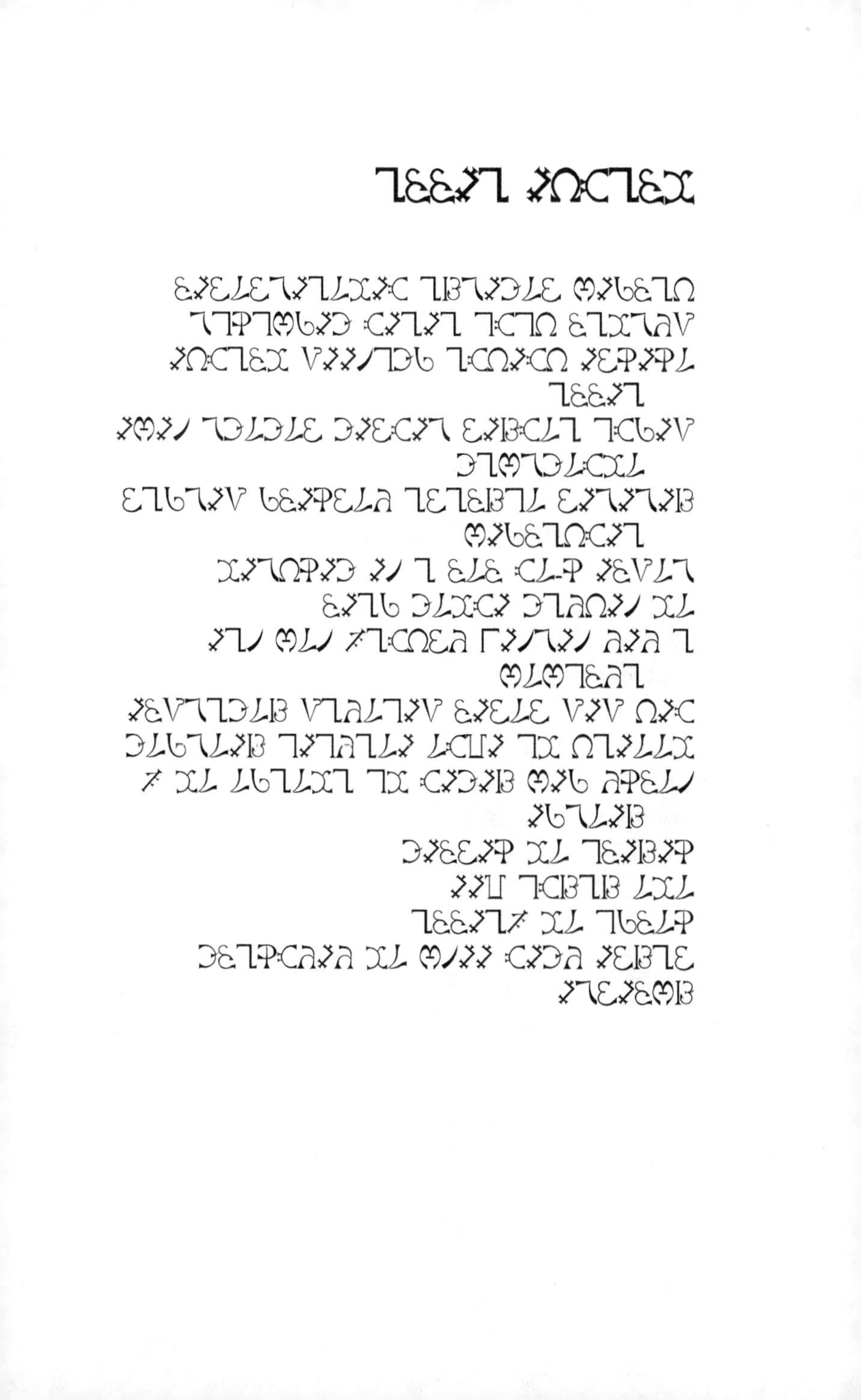

Drilpa Yarry

Pirgah Monasci ladoiasmomar!
Busdir PELE, iaial naghezes
ozazma plapli gnetaab Drilpa Yarry
bagle yolcam salman monons taha odlonshin
casasam oecrimi vomzarg basgim Ialpirgah
sobra z-ol ror i ta nazpsad
od tapuin aldon giar
i vau tastax umplif toh tia Iurehoh
lap bab momar baeovib conisbra
Dooaip de aqlo Aoiveae caosgon
torzu gah canal de Idoigo od f caosga
zacare od zamran
odo cicle qaa
zorge od fyarry
micma unal aath od vaulzirn
chramsa

Great Providence

Glory to the Great Name of God Is, Was, and Shall Be Crowned!
Glorious Worker of Wonders, conclude us to be worthy
to make us partakers in your governments of Great Providence
because to bring forth a house in the heart of triumph and powers
abiding to sing praises every day unto The Flames of the First Glory
in whose hands the sun is as a sword
and sickles to gather up the harvest
is to work going before the strength to triumph as unto What Christ Did In Hell
for the dominion to crown righteousness in the works of man
In the Name of your Stars unto the Earth
arise you continual workmen of He Who Sits on the Holy Throne and visit the earth
move and show your selves
open the mysteries of your creation
be friendly unto me and visit with providence
behold these deeds and work wonders
be it made with power

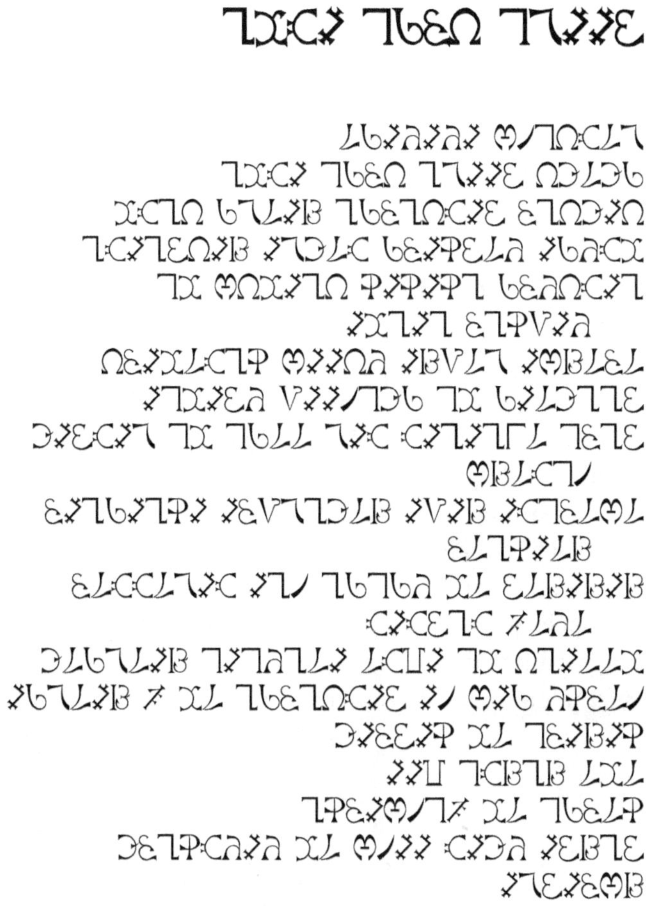

Maase Prge Aldi

Solpeth Avavago
gnonp maasi prge aldi
panpir malpirgi caosg pild
dluga vomzarg lonsa capmiali.
Ialpurg izazaz piadph de vabzir Iaida
orocha sobca upaah zilodarp
miinoag de gnetaab umadea
mire oxiayal las ooge de Salman Teloch.
Ohorela caba conisbra aziagiar coazior
cacacom od ugegi tia lasollor ovof limlal.
Dooaip de aqlo Aoiveae caosgon
torzu gah ta malpirgi od f caosga
zacare od zamran
odo cicle qaa
zorge od fetharzi
micma unal aath od vaulzirn
chramsa

Stored Fire of Gathering

Hearken unto the Thunders of Increase
garnished with the stored fire of gathering
pouring down the fires of life and increase upon the
earth continually
giving unto every one of you power successively.
The burning flames have framed within the depths of
the jaws of the eagle of the Highest
beneath whose wings stretch forth
the corners of your government's strong towers
upon the mighty seat in the rich chambers of the
House of the Dead.
Legislate to govern the work of man like unto a
harvest to increase
flourish and grow strong as unto a rich man magnifies
his treasure.
In the Name of your Stars unto the Earth
arise you spirits as fires of life and increase and visit
the earth
move and show your selves
open the mysteries of your creation
be friendly unto me and visit with peace
behold these deeds and work wonders
be it made with power

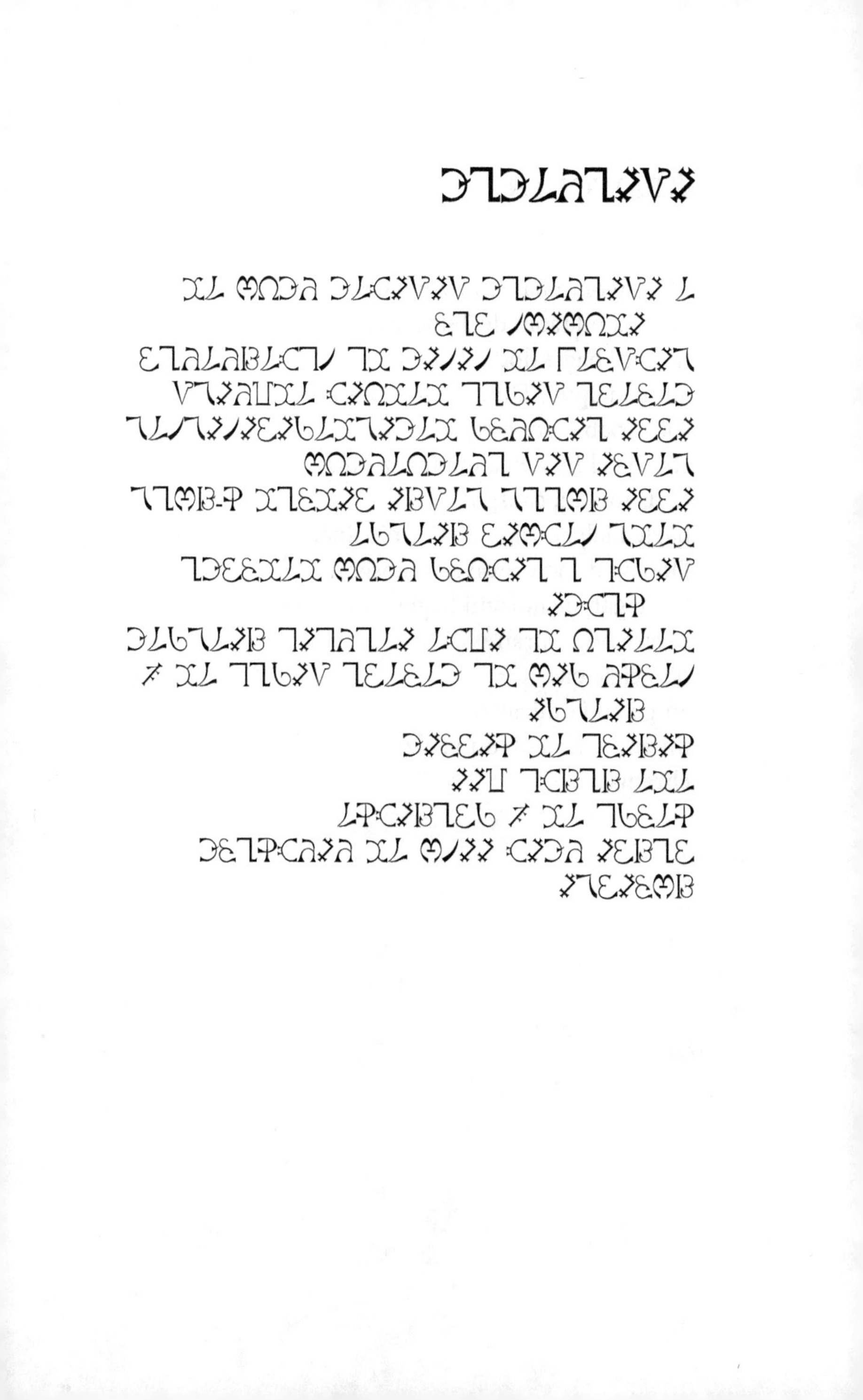

[illegible]

[illegible]
[illegible]
[illegible]
[illegible]
[illegible]
[illegible]
[illegible]
[illegible]
[illegible]
[illegible]
[illegible]
[illegible]
[illegible]
[illegible]
[illegible]
[illegible]
[illegible]
[illegible]

Abaivonin

O abaivonin babalon vnph od adphaht mir
salbrox od tatan de Telocvovim
noromi bagie dodpal odquasb
amma ialpurg Donasdogamatastos
sobra bab ivonpovnph.
Amma chiis sobca madrid z-chis
dods tolham caosgo
bagle i ialprg vnph dodrmni zilna.
Dooaip de aqlo Aoiveae caosgon
torzu gah de noromi bagie od f caosga
zacare od zamran
odo cicle qaa
zorge od f gmicalzo
micma unal aath od vaulzirn
chramsa

Stooping Dragons

Come bear witness to the stooping dragons of wicked
anger and unspeakable torment
the burning sulphur and wormwood of the Death
Dragon Who Is Fallen
o you sons of fury who vex and destroy
with the cursed burning flames of The Furious and
Perpetual Fire Enclosed for the Punishment of
Them That Are Banished From the Glory
whose domination is wrath in anger.
Cursed are they whose iniquities they are
vexing all creatures of the earth
for it is the burning flame of anger vexed in itself.
In the Name of your Stars unto the Earth
arise you spirits of the sons of fury and visit the earth
move and show your selves
open the mysteries of your creation
be friendly unto me and visit with power
behold these deeds and work wonders
be it made with power

[illegible] DRAGONS

Conjure [illegible] the creeping dragons [illegible]
empire and [illegible] formed
the [illegible] and [illegible] of the Dark
Dragon Who [illegible]
[illegible] who [illegible]
with [illegible] flames of the [illegible]
[illegible] enclosed [illegible]
[illegible] Earth [illegible]
[illegible] domination is [illegible]
[illegible] are they [illegible]
[illegible] of the earth
[illegible] the burning flame of [illegible]
In the Name of your [illegible] the Earth
arise you spirits of [illegible] and visit the earth
move and [illegible]
open the [illegible] of [illegible]
[illegible] visit [illegible]
[illegible]
[illegible] with power

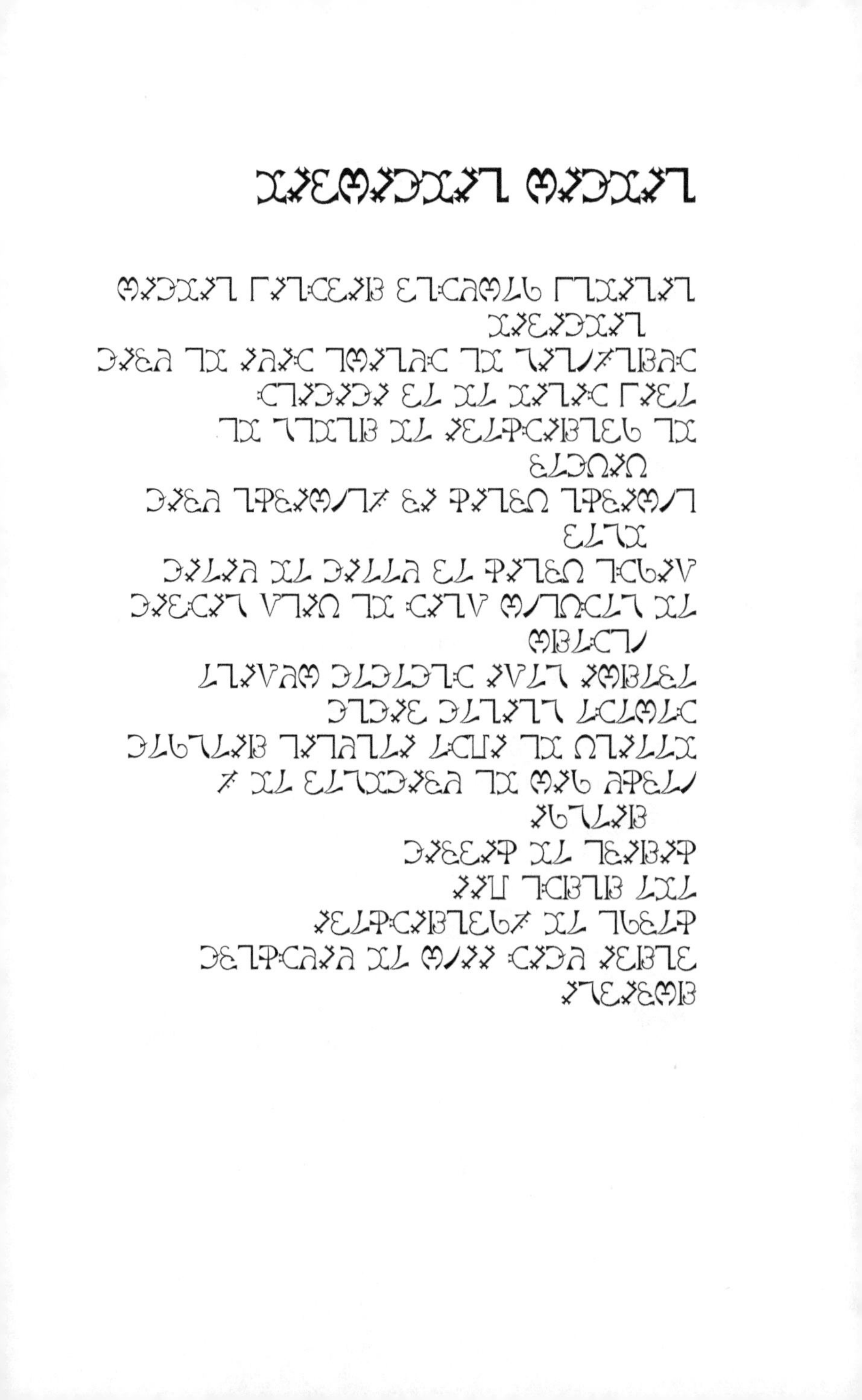

Iadnah Iadnahmad

Iaiadix, gohulim, camliax iadnah iadnamad
luciftias de luiahe laua de uran
omax laiad od om ananael
de gmicalzoma od cides de papnor.
Etharzi priaz ar fetharzi vran dsom
bagle priaz om vooan od vaoan
od solpeth bial de paeb Salman Teloch
orocha soba linonon hubaio
loholo siaion manin.
Dooaip de aqlo Aoiveae caosgon
torzu gah de Urandsom od f caosga
zacare od zamran
odo cicle qaa
zorge od fgmicalzoma
micma unal aath od vaulzirn
chramsa

Knowledge of Pure Knowledge

Honour, it is said, speaks of the knowledge of pure knowledge
the brightness of the song of honour in the humility of elders
to know the secrets of truth and understand the secret wisdom
of the power of understanding and the mysteries of memory.
Peace to those that visit in peace the elders that understand
for they understand lower-truth and higher-truth
and hearken the voicings of the oak in the House of Death
beneath whose branches lanterns
shine in the temple in the mind.
In the Name of your Stars unto the Earth
arise you spirits of Elders That Understand and visit the earth
move and show your selves
open the mysteries of your creation
be friendly unto me and visit with the power of understanding
behold these deeds and work wonders
be it made with power

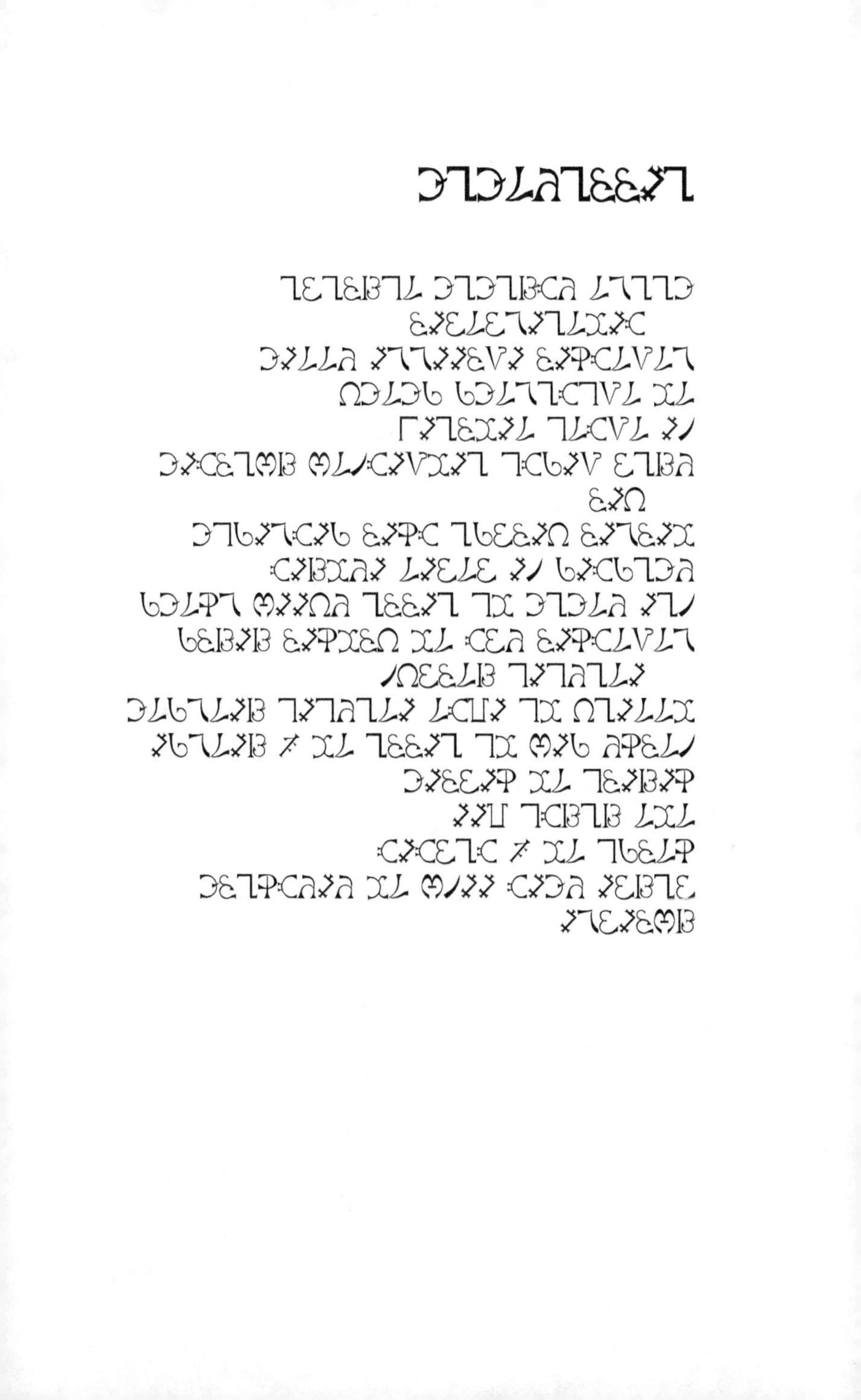

[illegible]

[illegible]
[illegible]
[illegible]
[illegible]
[illegible]
[illegible]
[illegible]
[illegible]
[illegible]
[illegible]
[illegible]
[illegible]
[illegible]
[illegible]
[illegible]
[illegible]
[illegible]
[illegible]
[illegible]

Yarryvonin

Niiso! Ulcinin oecrimi ladoiasmomar
sobolzar abraassa vooan
od obelisong gnonp
ta obloe oadriax
ucim bagle Iadbaltoh chirlan par
darsar parmgi lzar Galsagen
uniglag ta momao Audcal
tia vonin de yarry upaah szong
sobolzar uml od prdzar cacrg aoiveae cormpt.
Dooaip de aqlo Aoiveae caosgon
torzu gah de yarry od f caosga
zacare od zamran
odo cicle qaa
zorge od f limlal
micma unal aath od vaulzirn
chramsa

Providence Dragons

Come away! Happy is he who sings praises of God Is,
    Was, and Shall Be Crowned
whose courses provide the lower truth
and the pleasant deliverers to garnish
the garland of the lower heavens
frown not for the God of Righteousness rejoiceth in
    them
wherefore let run the courses of Divine Power
    Creating the Angel of the Sun
to descend as crowns of Alchemical Gold/Mercury
as unto dragons of providence on the wings of the
    winds,
whose courses add and diminish until the stars are
    numbered.
In the Name of your Stars unto the Earth
arise you spirits of providence and visit the earth
move and show your selves
open the mysteries of your creation
be friendly unto me and visit with treasure
behold these deeds and work wonders
be it made with power

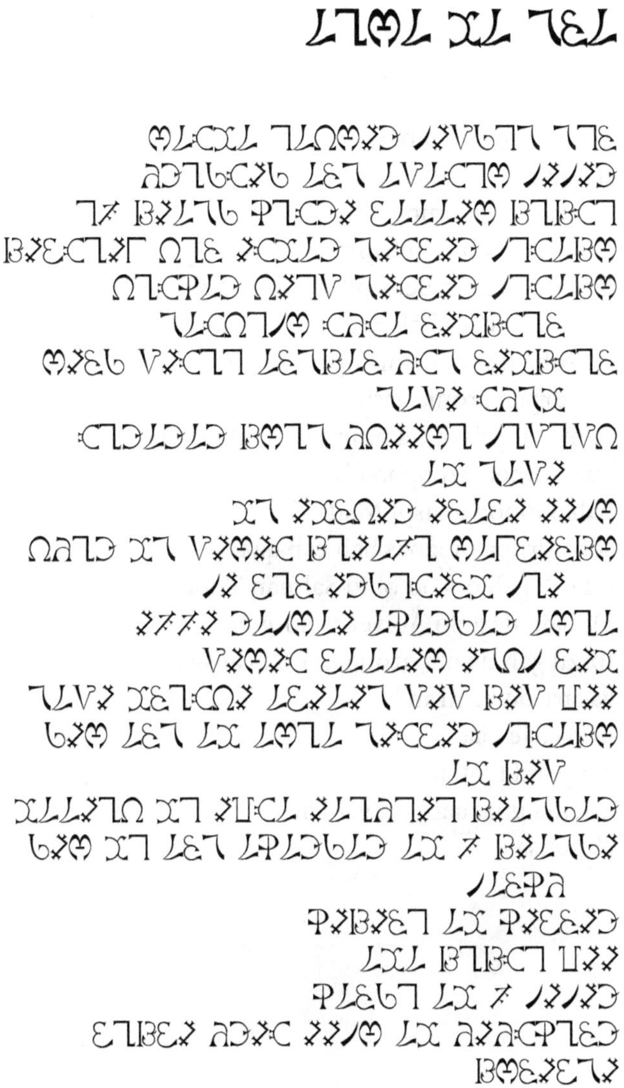

Ors Od Ohio

Holdo eophan tabges ser
uniglag ors oboleh tatan
ef caosg zylna moooah cicle
camliax pir aldon Salman Teloch.
Solpeth Lulo radclir pilzon paeb Salman Teloch
soba lusd harg balye orscor uls radclir
od soba linonon chis upaahi tibibp
ds adrpan aroma aath
ta mir angelard tia puin ds bahal ciaofi hoxmarch
affa nothoa ozongon ohio
bahal moooah aspt Mad
soba drilpa omaoas bab cab qaa
od cab gah ors od ohio Salman Teloch
Dooaip de aqlo Aoiveae caosgon
torzu gah de ors ozongon od f caosga
zacare od zamran
odo cicle qaa
zorge od f tatan
micma unal aath od vaulzirn
chramsa

Darkness and Woe

Groan a lamentation from the caves of sorrow
to descend into darkness in garments of wormwood
visit the earth within itself to repent the mysteries
spake by the spirits gathered in the House of Death.
Hearken to the Mother of Tartar who weeps to water
    the oak in the House of Death
whose feet are planted in the salt from the dryness at
    the ends of weeping
and whose branches are as wings of sorrow
which cast down cursed works
as a torment of thoughts as unto sickles that cry
    loudly the terror to fear god
empty amidst the manifold winds of woe
cry loudly to repent before Your Undefiled God
whose great names' dominion govern creation
and govern the spirits of darkness and woe in the
    House of Death.
In the Name of your Stars unto the Earth
arise you spirits of the dark and manifold winds and
    visit the earth
move and show your selves
open the mysteries of your creation
be friendly unto me and visit with wormwood
behold these deeds and work wonders
be it made with power

[illegible]

[illegible]
[illegible]
[illegible]
[illegible]
[illegible]
[illegible]
[illegible]
[illegible]
[illegible]
[illegible]
[illegible]
[illegible]
[illegible]
[illegible]
[illegible]
[illegible]
[illegible]
[illegible]

Pasbs de Pabliar

Turbs bliorax balit
camliax hoath soba monons mad moz
salman paradiz oecrimi
luiahe busdirtilb pasbs turbs
ds yolci limlal drilpi achildao.
Bagle abramig pibliar luciftian
od urbs oboleh de Qurlstoma
i cacacom tia lorslq ooge Idoigo
od oecrimi pambt qaa Gohed.
Dooaip de aqlo Aoiveae caosgon
torzu Pasbs de Pabliar od f caosga
zacare od zamran
odo cicle qaa
zorge od fturbs
micma unal aath od vaulzirn
chramsa

Daughters of the Places of Comfort

Beauty shalt comfort the just,
spake the true worshipper whose heart of undefiled
joy
is a house of virgins singing
a song of honour to the glory of Her daughters of
beauty
which bringeth forth treasures greater than diamond.
For to prepare places of comfort with ornaments of
brightness
and to beautify the garments of the Handmaidens of
Understanding
is to flourish as unto flowers in the chamber of Him
Who Sits upon the Holy Throne
and to sing praises unto the creation of The One
Everlasting.
In the Name of your Stars unto the Earth
arise you Daughters of the Places of Comfort and visit
the earth
move and show your selves
open the mysteries of your creation
be friendly unto me and visit with beauty
behold these deeds and work wonders
be it made with power

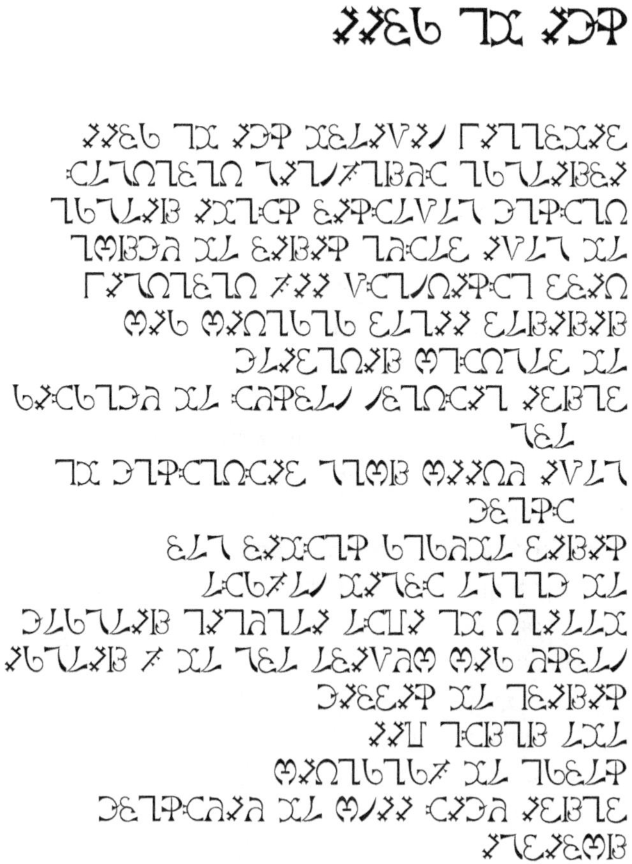

Zna De Graa

Madriiax, tabaord zna de graa
arcaosgi luciftias piripsol,
pilzin, sobolzar zlida caosgi
od soba molvi zacar od unchi
parm elzaptilb aaf piripsax
cacacom aaiom gigipah gah
od mospleh capimaon.
Micma ialpirt torzul od uniglag ors
soba upaah chis malpilzin de lzirn
zacam odugeg zildar sor
od niiso lrsad tofglo.
Dooaip de aqlo Aoiveae caosgon
torzu gah hubaro ors od f caosga
zacare od zamran
odo cicle qaa
zorge od fgigipah
micma unal aath od vaulzirn
chramsa

Motion of the Moon

Oh you heavens, be governed by the motion of the
Moon
to advance upon the Earth as the brightness of the
heavens,
the Firmament of Waters whose courses water the
earth
and whose surges to move and to confound
run her course amongst the heavens
to flourish amongst us the living breath of spirits
and the horns of the number of time.
Behold the light that shall rise and descend in the
darkness
whose wings are the through-thrusting waters of
wonders
move and wax strong to fly into regal action
and come away to dispose all things.
In the Name of your Stars unto the Earth
arise you spirits of living lamps in the darkness and
visit the earth
move and show your selves
open the mysteries of your creation
be friendly unto me and visit with living breath
behold these deeds and work wonders
be it made with power

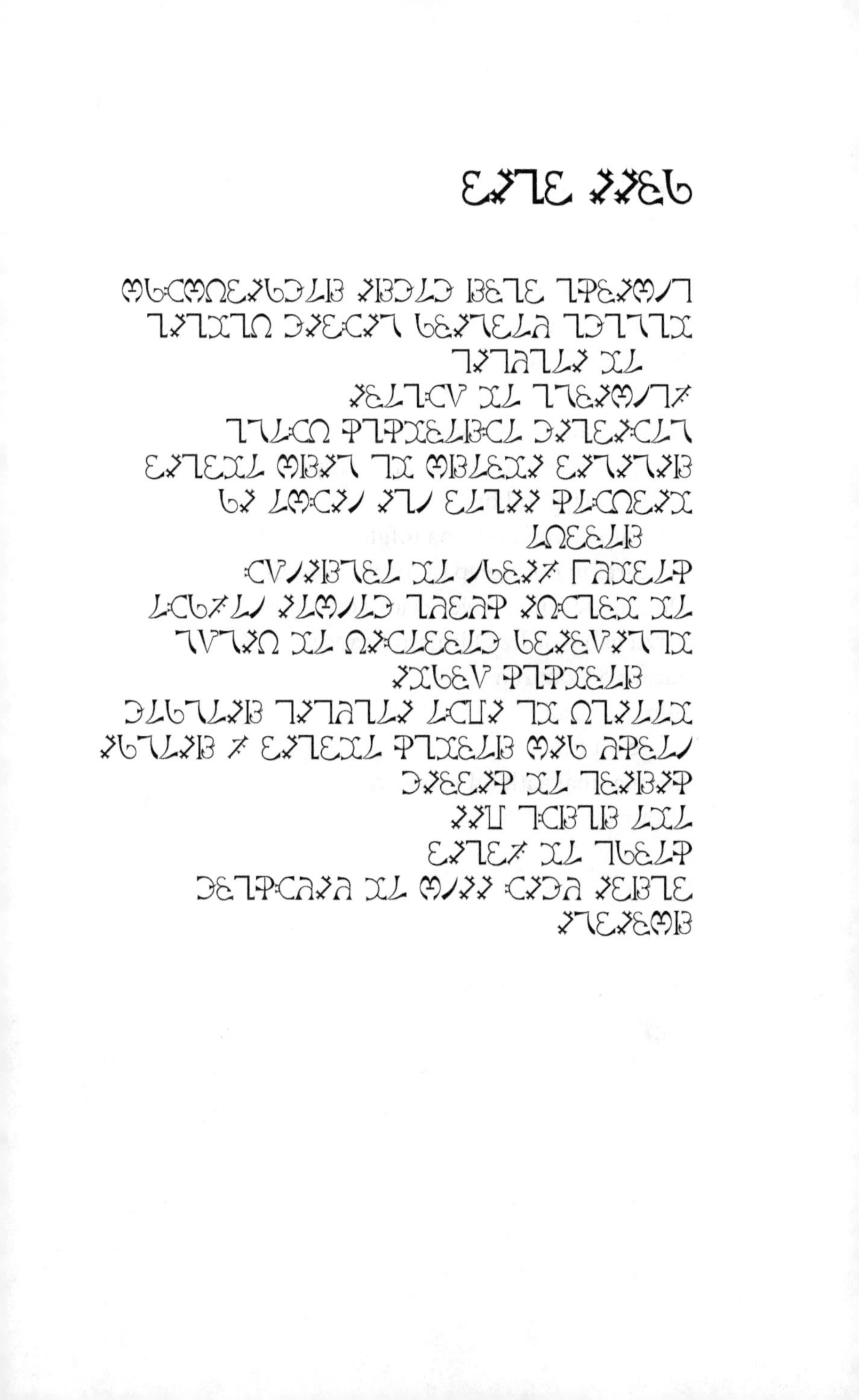

[illegible]

[illegible]
[illegible]
[illegible]
[illegible]
[illegible]
[illegible]
[illegible]
[illegible]
[illegible]
[illegible]
[illegible]
[illegible]
[illegible]
[illegible]
[illegible]
[illegible]
[illegible]
[illegible]
[illegible]

Graa Miam

Etharzi mirc nonca Congamphlgh Graa Miam
disini vomsarg salman pidiai od aoiveae
fetharsi od bliora
Solamian Olcordziz plosi
casasam adroch de Sach Odmiam
damploz aaiom tia talho ag cormpo
zomdux fargt od orscatbl
od drilpa zumvi nothoa tofglo
desabramg normolap od pasbs cordziz brgda.
Dooaip de aqlo Aoiveae caosgon
torzu gah Cordiz Odmiam f caosga
zacare od zamran
odo cicle qaa
zorge od fmiam
micma unal aath od vaulzirn
chramsa

MOON'S CONTINUANCE

Peace be upon you by Faith in the Moon's
 Continuance
which walkest through every house of marble and
 stars
to visit us in peace and comfort
Whose Continuance has made Mankind as many
abiding in the olive mount of The Establishers and
 Continuance
variety amongst us as unto cups none hath yet
 numbered
encompassed by dwelling places and buildings
and the great seas amidst all things
which are prepared for the sons of men and the
 daughters of mankind to sleep.
In the Name of your Stars unto the Earth
arise you spirits of Mankind and Continuance to visit
 the earth
move and show your selves
open the mysteries of your creation
be friendly unto me and visit with continuance
behold these deeds and work wonders
be it made with power

[illegible]

[illegible] CONTINUANCE

Praise be to you, the Lord in the Mounts [illegible]
[illegible]
[illegible] every house of [illegible] and
[illegible]

[illegible] comfort
[illegible] Mansion [illegible]
and [illegible] of The Establishers and
[illegible]

[illegible] more hallowed
[illegible]

encompasses [illegible] places and buildings
and the great seas [illegible] all things
[illegible] the sons of man and the
[illegible] to them
In the name of [illegible] unto the Earth
[illegible] and Continuance to you
[illegible]

[illegible] ourselves
[illegible] creation
[illegible] with [illegible]
[illegible] these [illegible] and work wonders
[illegible] made [illegible]

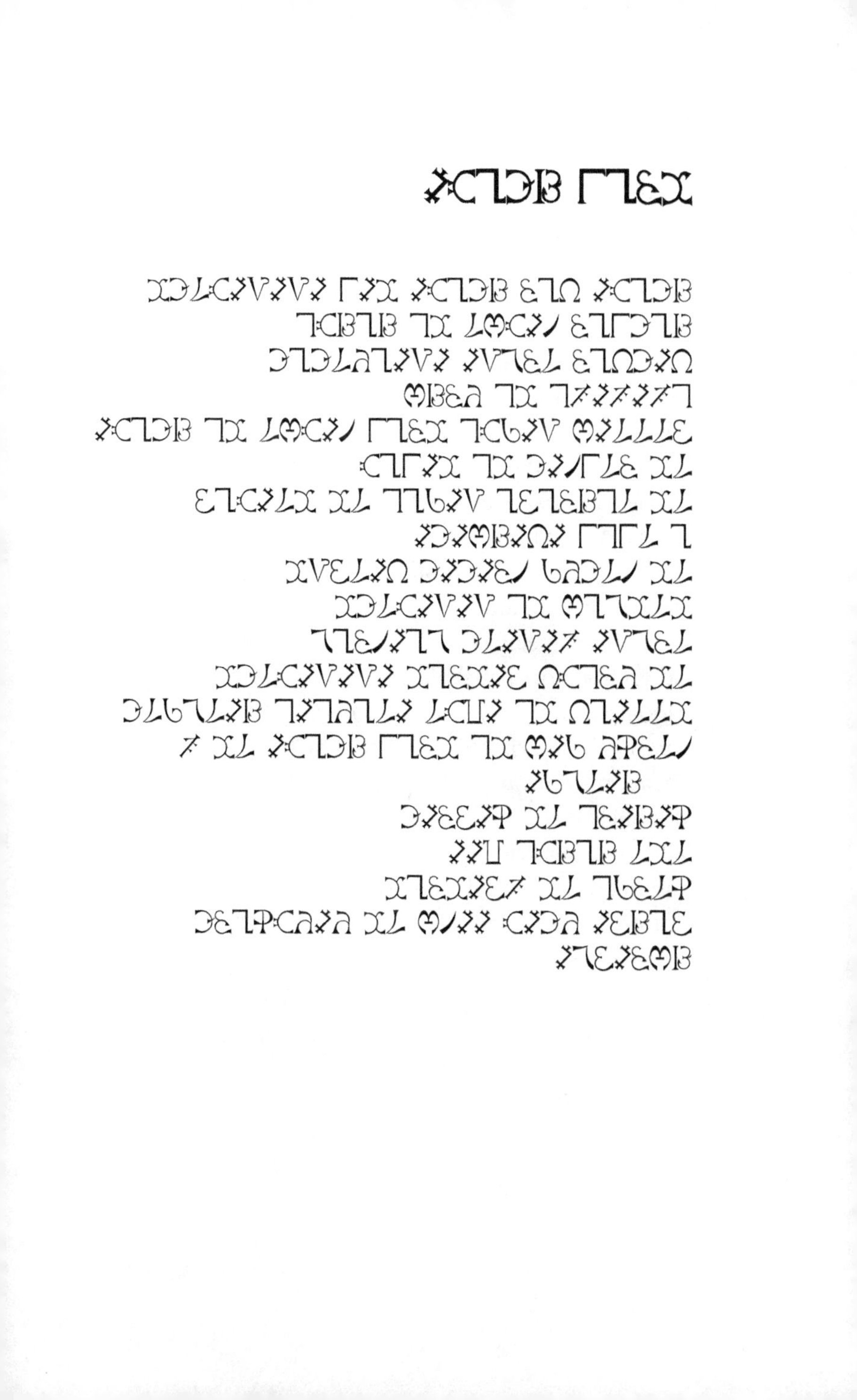

Drix Cnila

Cnila pir, cnila dax ababalond
cinxir talho de cicle
panpir orsba abaivonin
efafafe de urch.
Moooah! Bagle drix talho de cnila
od roxtan de daxil
od oecrimi bagie od doalim
i oxex Apachana
od tonug tranan paombd
dodsih de babalond
orsba fabaon siatris
od vrelp madrid ababalond.
Dooaip de aqlo Aoiveae caosgon
torzu gah de drix cnila od f caosga
zacare od zamran
odo cicle qaa
zorge od fmadrid
micma unal aath od vaulzirn
chramsa

Cast Down Blood

Blood from the holy ones, blood from the loins of the
harlot
mingle in the cups of mysteries
pour down drunken stooping dragons
from vials of the Confusers.
Repent! For to cast down cups of blood
and the rectified wine of your loins
and to sing praises of fury and sin
is to vomit the Slimy Things Made of Dust
and to deface the marrow of appendages
in vexation of the wicked
drunken on the poison of scorpions
and the strongly seething iniquity in harlots.
In the Name of your Stars unto the Earth
arise you spirits of cast down blood and visit the earth
move and show your selves
open the mysteries of your creation
be friendly unto me and visit with iniquity
behold these deeds and work wonders
be it made with power

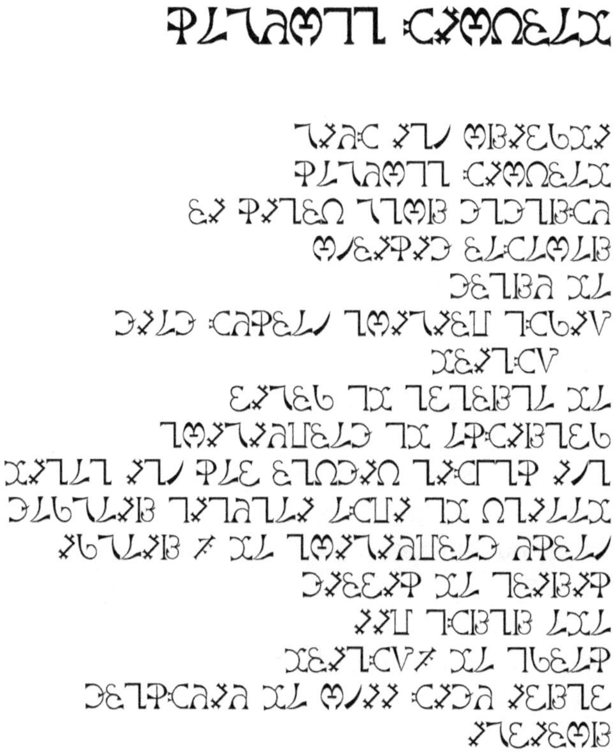

Dorphal Iehusoz

Adgmach tia Luas
dorphal Iehusoz!
Ulcinin chis priaz ar
coholor Nazarth
od ucirn
bagle qrasahi torzul noan bliard
od oecrimi de grsam
gmicalzo de Norquasahi
ita zixlay panpir moz tia Ioiad!
Dooaip de aqlo Aoiveae caosgon
torzu Norquasahi od f caosga
zacare od zamran
odo cicle qaa
zorge od fbliard
micma unal aath od vaulzirn
chramsa

Looking with Gladness upon God's Mercies

Praise as unto Those Who Praise
looking with Gladness upon God's Mercies!
Happy are those that
lift up Pillars of Gladness
and frown not
for pleasure shall rise to become comfort
and to sing praises of admiration
in power of the Sons of Pleasure
is as to stir up to pour down joy as unto Him That
    Liveth Forever!
In the Name of your Stars unto the Earth
arise you Sons of Pleasure and visit the earth
move and show your selves
open the mysteries of your creation
be friendly unto me and visit with comfort
behold these deeds and work wonders
be it made with power

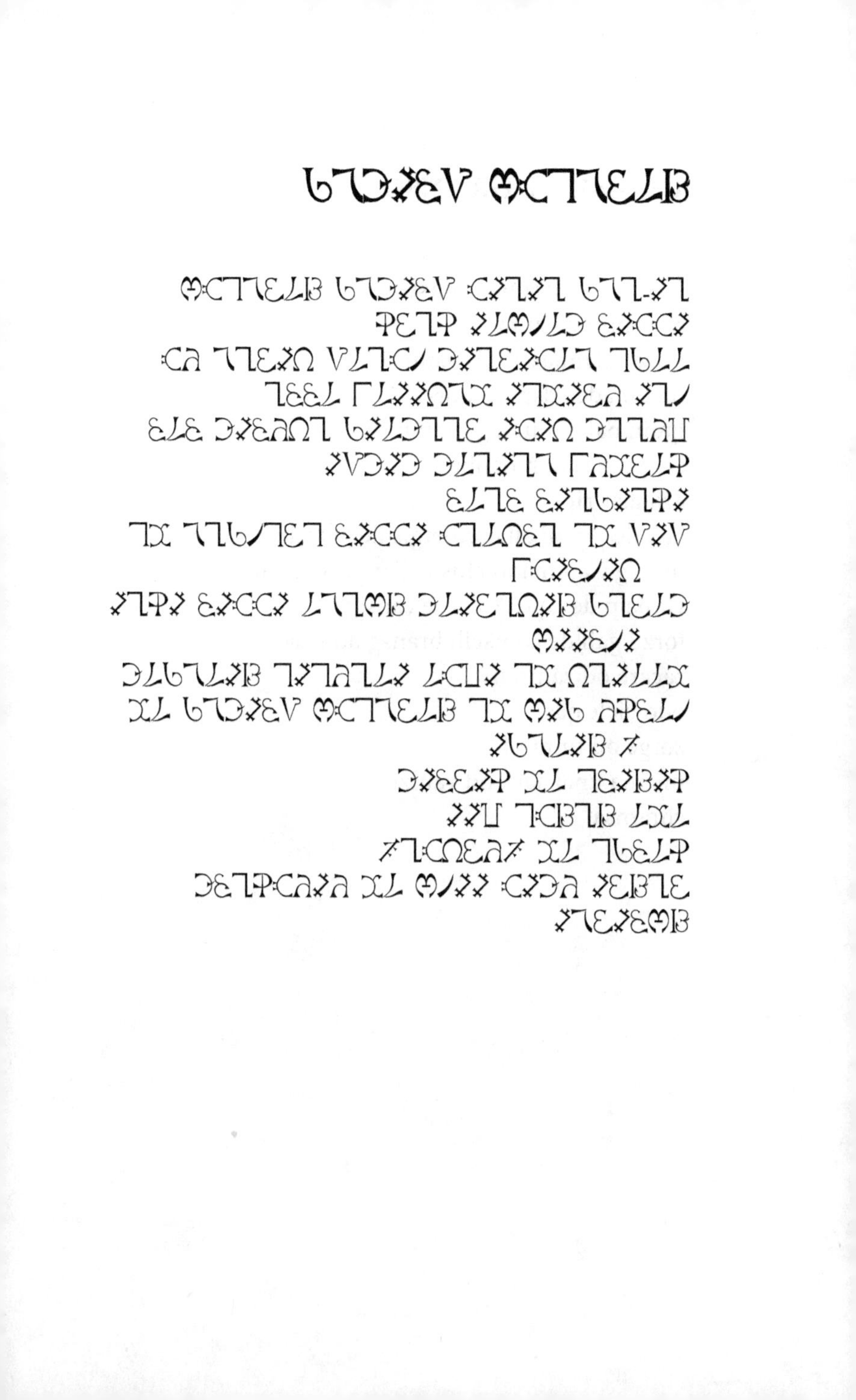

[illegible]

[illegible]
[illegible]
[illegible]
[illegible]
[illegible]
[illegible]
[illegible]
[illegible]
[illegible]
[illegible]
[illegible]
[illegible]
[illegible]
[illegible]
[illegible]
[illegible]
[illegible]
[illegible]
[illegible]

Comselh Bransg

Ia-isg, iaial bransg comselh
allar nothoa zimz
ooge solamian tliob pamis ul
tia umadea dspaaox orri
quiin pala miinoag ipuran ror
zomdux siaion nanba
aziagiar rior
bab de yrpoil allar emetgis de patralx
nomig Capimaon chiso allar azia atraah.
Dooaip de aqlo Aoiveae caosgon
torzu gah de comselh bransg od f caosga
zacare od zamran
odo cicle qaa
zorge od fumplif
micma unal aath od vaulzirn
chramsa

Circle Guard

Everlasting One and Indivisible God, conclude this
guard circle
to bind up amidst territories
a chamber whose continuance to separate creatures
cannot end
as unto strong towers which remain barren stone
wherein two separated by corner-boundaries shall not
see the sun
encompassed by a temple of thorns
as unto the harvest of a widow
a dominion of division bound up as a seal of rock
even as the Number of Time shall be bound up like
unto your girdles.
In the Name of your Stars unto the Earth
arise you spirits of the circle guard and visit the earth
move and show your selves
open the mysteries of your creation
be friendly unto me and visit with strength
behold these deeds and work wonders
be it made with power

CIRCLE GUARD

…lasting One and Indivisible God, conclude the …
…eternal circle …
…ding up similar territories
…chumbe who … nature are by separate creatures
…rcadano cha…
…ts … powers wh… remain …
… … impartial … shall …
…dynasty
…ation … of the …
… the harvest … awaiting
… dominion of … bound … of rock
even as the … of … like
… under your guidance …
In the … of your S… onto the Earth.
… spirits of the … and visit the …
… snow-… …
… the mystery …
… … and visit …
… …
… …

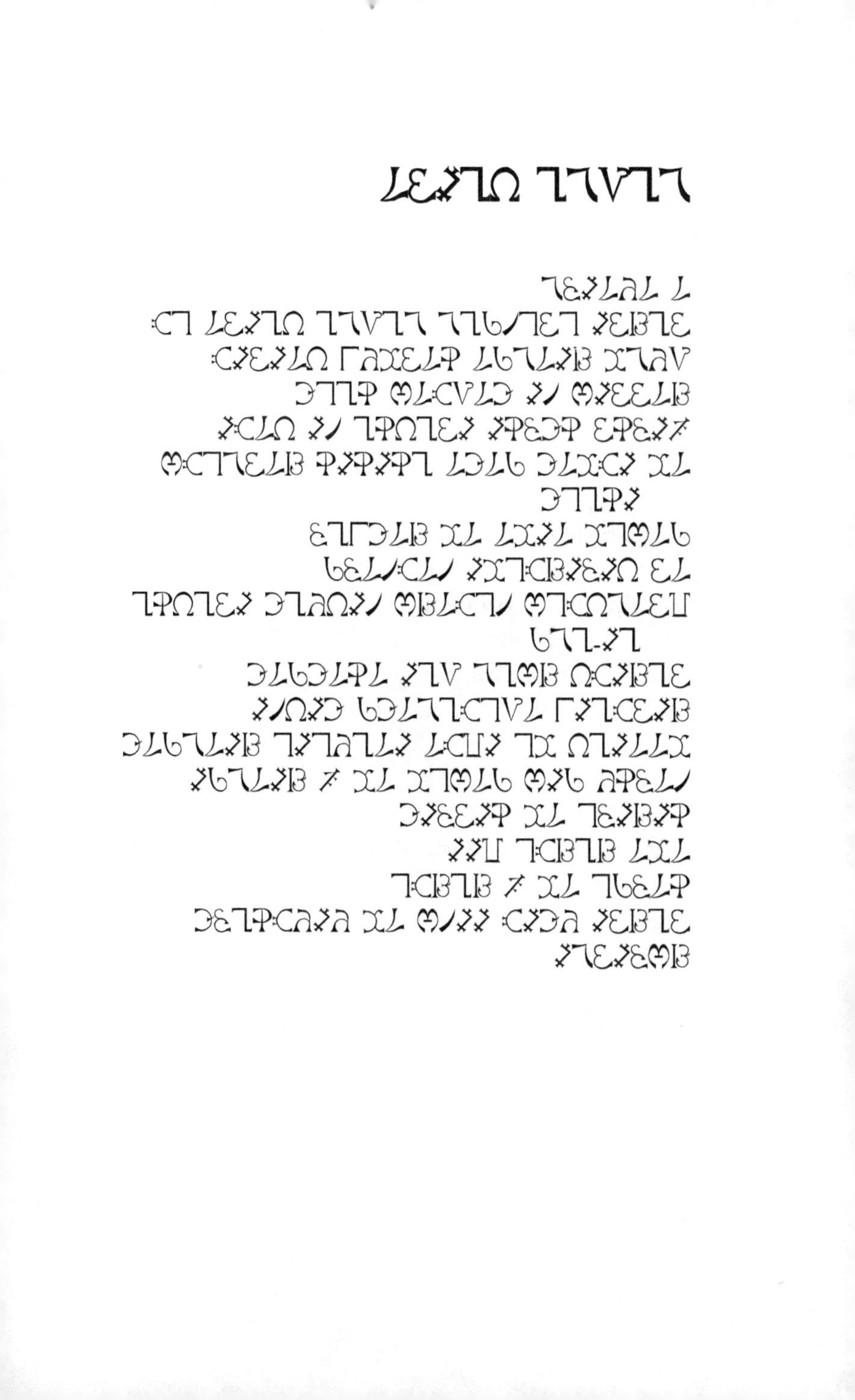

Sibsi Piamo

O ovoars!
Micma emetgis sibsi piamo el
busd caosgo zomdux poamal
commah ta nobloh zien
farzm znrza amipzi ta pola
od aldon gono izazaz comselh azien
Gohed oado od conxir
om paracleda toltorg
qmospleh teloch tapvin amipzi Ja-isg.
Micalp chis bia ozongon
camliax obelisong napta.
Dooaip de aqlo Aoiveae caosgon
torzu gah Gohed od f caosga
zacare od zamran
odo cicle qaa
zorge od f cicle
micma unal aath od vaulzirn
chramsa

Covenant at the Balance of Righteousness

Come and bear witness at the center!
Behold the seal of covenant at the balance of
    righteousness
the glory of the earth in the midst of your palace
to truss together as the palms of my hands
you lifted up your voices and swore to fasten as two-
    coupled-together
and gather together faith to form a circle on whose
    hands
All Things Descending Upon One weaves and mingles
the understanding of the wedding of the creatures of
    the earth
or the horns of death that fasten us to the Everlasting
    One and Indivisible God.
Mightier are your voices than the manifold winds
speaking as pleasant deliverers with two edged
    swords.
In the Name of your Stars unto the Earth
arise you spirits of All Things Descending Upon One
    and visit the earth
move and show your selves
open the mysteries of your creation
be friendly unto me and visit with mysteries
behold these deeds and work wonders
be it made with power

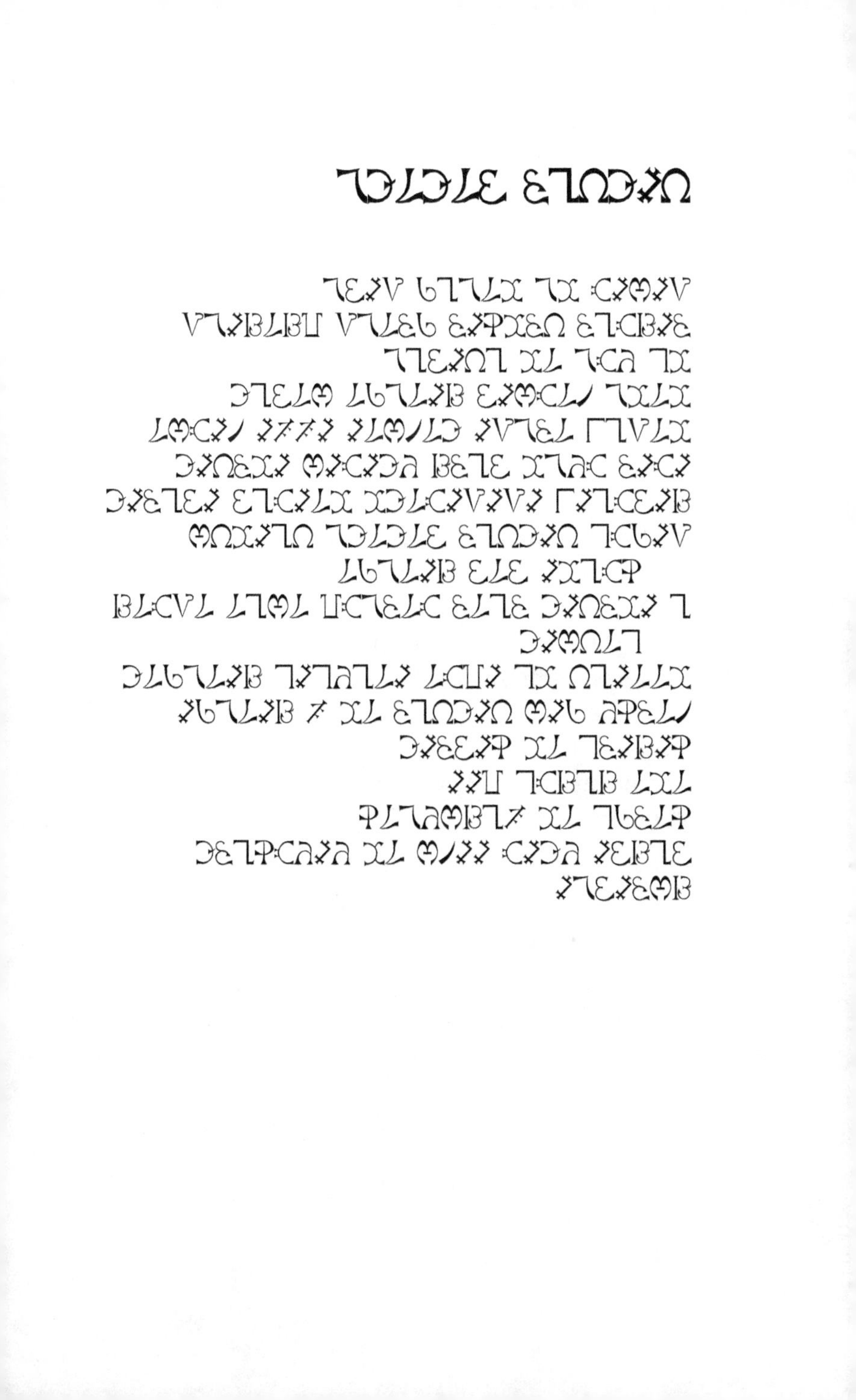

[illegible]

[illegible]
[illegible]
[illegible]
[illegible]
[illegible]
[illegible]
[illegible]
[illegible]
[illegible]
[illegible]
[illegible]
[illegible]
[illegible]
[illegible]
[illegible]
[illegible]
[illegible]
[illegible]

Panpir Monons

Bahal ds dosig bams!
Raclir prdzar grosb qcocasb
de uls od ipamis
dods tolham caosgo homin
dobix orsba nothoa affa talho
alar lusd mirc unalah adrpan
camliax ababalond doalim amiran
bagle panpir monons piadph zlida mom caosgo
i adrpan rior lorslq ohio obloc eophan.
Dooaip de aqlo Aoiveae caosgon
torzu gah panpir od f caosga
zacare od zamran
odo cicle qaa
zorge od fichusoz
micma unal aath od vaulzirn
chramsa

Pouring Out the Heart

Cry with a loud voice of that which night forgets!
Weeping to diminish the bitter sting of the contents of time
of ends and what can not be
vexing all creatures of the earth with age
to fall drunken amidst empty cups
and set your feet upon your skirts cast down
speaking with a harlot of the sin of yourselves
for to pour out your heart from the depths of your jaws to water the moss of the earth
is to cast down widow's flowers of woe from a garland of lamentation
In the Name of your Stars unto the Earth
arise you spirits who pour out and visit the earth
move and show your selves
open the mysteries of your creation
be friendly unto me and visit with His mercies
behold these deeds and work wonders
be it made with power

[illegible] HEART

[illegible] the loudvoice of [illegible] might [illegible]
[illegible] the [illegible] the fragments of
[illegible]
[illegible] ends and [illegible]
[illegible] and [illegible]

[illegible]

[illegible] the Earth
[illegible] with the [illegible]
[illegible]

[illegible] with [illegible]
[illegible]

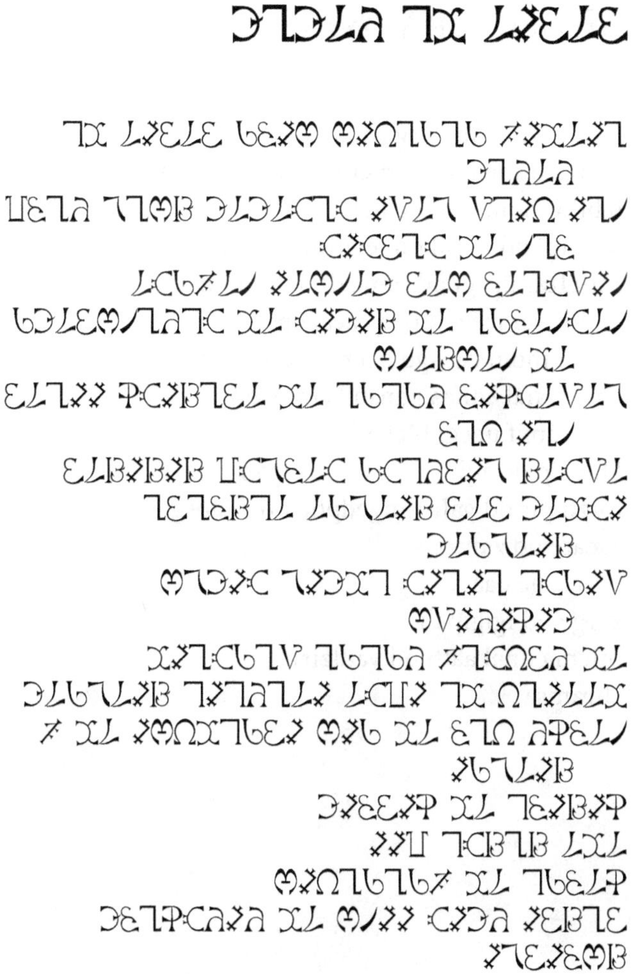

Momao de Vonin

Iaodaf gigipah harg Momao de Vovin
tia paeb soba lilonon chis virq rit od limlal
tablior hom nothoa tofglo
toltorgi od canal od levithmong od tohcoth
sobolzar ugegi od omicalz aaiom tia pir.
Obloc samvelg lorslq cacacom
aldon mom caosgo oecrimi caosgon
bagle iaial ednas Lansh Nazavabh
od umplif ugegi bigliad.
Dooaip de aqlo Aoiveae caosgon
torzu pir od gah Amgedpha od f caosga
zacare od zamran
odo cicle qaa
zorge od fgigipah
micma unal aath od vaulzirn
chramsa

Crowns of the Dragon

In the Beginning the living breath hath planted
Crowns of the Dragon
as unto an oak whose branches are nests of mercy and
treasure
as comforters to live amidst all things
with creatures and continual workmen and the beasts
of the field and spirits of nature
whose courses waxeth strong and be mighty amongst
us as unto the holy ones.
A garland to the righteous who hath planted flowers
to flourish
and gathered up the moss of the earth to sing praises
unto the earth
for this concludes us receivers of the Exalted Power of
the Pillars of Hyacinth
and our strength waxeth strong in our Comforter.
In the Name of your Stars unto the Earth
arise you holy ones and spirits of I Will Begin Anew
and visit the earth
move and show your selves
open the mysteries of your creation
be friendly unto me and visit with living breath
behold these deeds and work wonders
be it made with power

[illegible]

I. [illegible]
[illegible]
[illegible]
[illegible]
[illegible]

II. [illegible]
[illegible]
[illegible]
[illegible]
[illegible]
[illegible]
[illegible]

III. [illegible]
[illegible]
[illegible]
[illegible]
[illegible]
[illegible]
[illegible]
[illegible]

Micmax-Ulx-Quasbx

I. Micmax
Micma drix cnila
crip toatar ip madrid
lap ti tianta babalond
od brita qting omp

II. Ulx
Niis ip! Brita ip! Iaial ip ednas babalon angelard
ag bab ge babalon bab panpir orsba doalim
affa ozien ananael pir
zonrensg cab erm iadnah

III. Quasbx
Tonug odquasb qting
lansh drixcnila
ta mir babalon
givi chis lusd
micalzo pilzin
ol aldonbliora od ugegi
aspt aldi Iadnamad

Beholding-Ending-Destroying

I. Beholding
Behold cast down blood
but hearken not the iniquity
for it is the bed of a harlot
and speaks rotten understanding

II. Ending
Come not! Speak not! Conclude us not receivers of
wicked thoughts
let no wicked dominion pour down drunken sin
empty mine own hand by the wisdom of the holy ones
who delivered a rod along with the ark of knowledge

III. Destroying
Deface and destroy the rotten
in power exalted above cast-down blood
as a torment to the wicked
stronger are your feet
mighty in the firmaments of water
I gather comfort and grow strong
before the gathering of pure knowledge

[illegible]

[illegible]
[illegible]
[illegible]
[illegible]

Oecrimi Gah Od Pir

oecrimi gah od pir
sobam zimz oiaida
soba camliax obelisong
de iadnamad od gmicalzoma

To Sing Praises to the Spirits and Holy Ones

to sing praises to the spirits and holy ones
who are the very garments of the highest
who speak as pleasant deliverers
of pure knowledge and the power of understanding

www.ingramcontent.com/pod-product-compliance
Lightning Source LLC
Chambersburg PA
CBHW071103090426
42737CB00013B/2460
* 9 7 8 1 9 1 4 1 6 6 4 5 7 *